To:

_____

You are one of the best things to happen in 1984.

And, as you are about to discover - a whole bunch of other historic events occurred in 1984 too! Enjoy!

Best wishes from:

_____

"Not merely the validity of experience, but
the very existence of external reality was
tacitly denied by their philosophy.'

'1984 - George Orwell'

EVENTS THAT TOOK PLACE IN JANUARY

Top Songs across the UK and USA charts this month:

United States: Say Say Say - Paul McCartney & Michael Jackson
United Kingdom: Only You - Flying Pickets

Events that took place in the UK

General Motors ends the manufacture of the Vauxhall Chevette.

After a solid nine-year run, General Motors bid farewell to the Vauxhall Chevette.

Brunei gains independence from the United Kingdom.

Brunei stepped into a new era, gaining independence from the UK after being a British protectorate since 1888.

The FTSE 100 Index begins.

The world of finance witnessed the inception of the FTSE 100 Index, changing the face of the UK stock market.

● **Left-wing MP Tony Benn wins the Labour Party's selection for the Chesterfield by-election.**

Benn made a strong comeback by securing the Labour Party's nod for the Chesterfield by-election, months after his electoral defeat in Bristol.

● **GCHQ staff are legally prevented from taking part in a Worker's Guild.**

A legal blockade emerged, preventing GCHQ staff from joining a Worker's Guild, adding a twist to union dynamics.

● **Nationwide Building Society introduces its first cash machine in the UK making a leap into modern banking.**

● **The Society of Motor Manufacturers and Traders declares that a record of almost 1.8 million cars were sold in Britain the previous year.**

The best selling car of 1983 was the Ford Escort.

THE MUSIC THAT SHAPED
THE UK IN 1984

1. *Relax by Frankie Goes To Hollywood*

2. *Two Tribes by Frankie Goes To Hollywood*

3. *I Just Called To Say I Love You by Stevie Wonder*

4. *Hello by Lionel Richie*

5. *Careless Whisper by George Michael*

6. *Agadoo by Black Lace*

7. *Ghostbusters by Ray Parker Jr*

8. *I Feel For You by Chaka Khan*

9. *The Reflex by Duran Duran*

10. *Freedom by Wham!*

Events that took place in the US

● The launch of the Apple Macintosh, the first personal computer
to feature a graphical user interface.

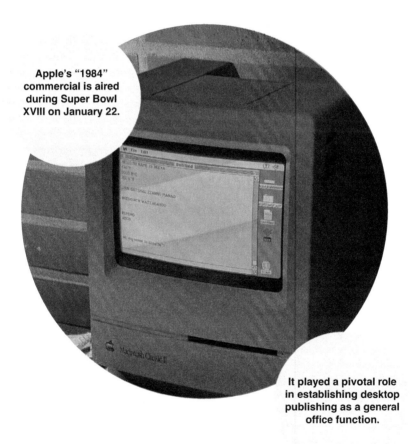

Apple's "1984" commercial is aired during Super Bowl XVIII on January 22.

It played a pivotal role in establishing desktop publishing as a general office function.

US President Ronald Reagan meets with Navy Lt Robert Goodman and the Rev Jesse Jackson at the White House following Lieutenant Goodman's release from Syrian incarceration.

Lieutenant Goodman was captured on December 4, 1983, during a bombing raid against Syrian anti-aircraft positions in Lebanon.

The US Bell System was split up.

AT&T's local phone service was divided into seven smaller companies, often referred to as Baby Bells. This division provided consumers with a broader range of options and reduced costs for long-distance calls and telephones.

Michael Jackson's hair catches fire during the taping of a Pepsi advert.

During the commercial's filming, pyrotechnics went off too early and set the legendary pop star's hair on fire.

Wilson Goode confirmed as Philadelphia's first black mayor.

He served from 1984 to 1992, a period which included the controversial MOVE police action and house bombing in 1985.

Ray 'Boom Boom' Mancini scores a third-round TKO of Bobby Chacon to hold his WBA lightweight title in Reno, Nevada. Chacon is so severely battered that he thanks referee Richard Steele for halting the fight.

Adrian Dantley ties Wilt Chamberlain's NBA record for most free tosses made in a game by converting 28 of 29 free tosses in Utah's 116–111 win over Houston at Las Vegas.

The US Supreme Court rules that private use of home VCRs to tape TV shows for later viewing does not violate government copyright laws.

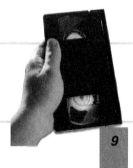

THE MUSIC THAT SHAPED
THE US IN 1984

1. *When Doves Cry / 17 Days by Prince*

2. *The Killing Moon / Do It Clean by Echo & The Bunnymen*

3. *William, It Was Really Nothing / Please Please Please Let Me Get What I Want by The Smiths*

4. *Purple Rain / God by Prince and The Revolution*

5. *Let's Go Crazy / Erotic City by Prince and The Revolution*

6. *Heaven Knows I'm Miserable Now / Suffer Little Children by The Smiths*

7. *What Difference Does It Make? / Back To The Old House by The Smiths*

8. *Pink Frost / Purple Girl by The Chills*

9. *For Whom the Bell Tolls by Metallica*

10. *I Will Dare / 20th Century Boy / Hey Good Lookin (Live) by The Replacements*

EVENTS THAT TOOK PLACE IN FEBRUARY

Top Songs across the UK and USA charts this month:

United States: Karma Chameleon - Culture Club
United Kingdom: Relax - Frankie goes to Hollywood

Events that took place in the UK

● Japanese car-maker Nissan comes to an agreement with the British government to create a factory in Britain.

This milestone arrangement means that 'foreign' vehicles will be made on British soil for the first time, with the industrial facility set to open in 1986.

End of the halfpenny!

Chancellor of the Exchequer Nigel Lawson declares that after 13 years, the halfpenny will be pulled from circulation.

● Satirical puppet show Spitting Image debuts on ITV, taking the television world by storm, offering a humorous and biting commentary on the era's politics and celebrities.

● **Great Britain and Northern Ireland take part in the Winter Olympics in Sarajevo, Yugoslavia.**

Torvill and Dean win a gold medal for ice dancing at the Winter Olympics.

13

Events that took place in the US

The first human embryo transfer from one woman to another resulted in a live birth.

This opened new doors for reproductive medicine, offering hope to countless couples struggling with infertility.

Space Shuttle Challenger is sent on the tenth space shuttle mission.

The Challenger made history with its triumphant landing at the Kennedy Space Centre - a first for any shuttle.

● Bill Johnson becomes the first American male to win an Olympic gold in alpine skiing at the Sarajevo Winter Olympics.

● Michael Jackson wins a record eight Grammy Awards.

These accolades recognised his iconic "Thriller" album, which became the best-selling album of all time.

● US Marines moved out of Beirut, Lebanon: marking a pivotal moment in the region's complex history. Their departure came after a challenging peacekeeping mission.

15

EVENTS THAT TOOK PLACE IN MARCH

Top Songs across the UK and USA charts this month:

United States: Jump - Van Halen
United Kingdom: 99 Red Balloons - Nena

Events that took place in the UK

● **Labour MP Tony Benn is back in parliament after winning the Chesterfield by-election, having lost his past seat at the general election the previous year, becoming a beacon of hope for many in the Labour Party.**

Only five months into being Labour Party leader, his party are elated when Labour comes top of a MORI survey with **41% of the vote** (in contrast to the 38% achieved by the Conservatives). This three-point lead over the Conservatives was a significant shift from just half a year prior when they trailed by a whopping 16 points.

The miners' strike starts and pits the National Union of Mineworkers against Margaret Thatcher's Conservative government.

The heart of the dispute? The government's decision to shutter the majority of Britain's remaining coal pits, a move that threatened livelihoods and communities.

Starlight Express opens at the Apollo Victoria Theatre in London.

This mesmerising musical on wheels captivated audiences, adding another gem to London's illustrious West End.

Sinn Fein's Gerry Adams and three others are hurt in an attack by the Ulster Volunteer Force (UVF), a loyalist paramilitary group.

This incident underscored the volatile political landscape of Northern Ireland during the Troubles.

Events that took place in the US

● CIA operative William Francis Buckley, is snatched by the Islamic Jihad and later dies in captivity.

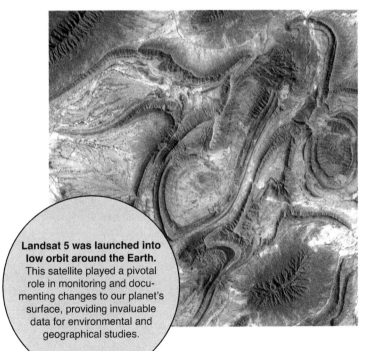

Landsat 5 was launched into low orbit around the Earth. This satellite played a pivotal role in monitoring and documenting changes to our planet's surface, providing invaluable data for environmental and geographical studies.

19

Tennis legend Martina Navratilova retains her WTA Tour Championship in New York beating Chris Evert for her fifth overall Championship title.

Hollywood's Shining Stars: Clint Eastwood, Burt Reynolds, Meryl Streep, Tom Selleck and Linda Evans win TV & Movie awards.

In a devastating environmental mishap, an oil tanker released a staggering 200,000 gallons of oil into the pristine waters of the Columbia River, threatening the river's ecosystem.

EVENTS THAT TOOK PLACE IN APRIL

Top Songs across the UK and USA charts this month:

United States: Footloose - Kenny Loggins
United Kingdom: Hello - Lionel Richie

Events that took place in the UK

● Over 100 pickets are involved in vicious conflicts at the Creswell colliery in Derbyshire and the Babbington colliery in Nottinghamshire.

It is the government's intention to close 20 coal mines across Britain.

Arthur Scargill, leader of the National Union of Mineworkers, holds a national ballot of miners on whether to proceed with their national strike, which has continued for five weeks.

● Tommy Cooper, a beloved comedian and magician, dies tragically from a heart attack in front of an audience during a live broadcast show, Live from Her Majesty's, aged 63.

● **WPC Yvonne Fletcher is shot and murdered by a sniper at the Libyan Embassy in London.**

In the wake of Yvonne Fletcher's murder, Britain cuts off ties with Libya and orders the remaining Libyan diplomats to depart the country.

● **The Greenham Common Women's Peace Camp, a symbol of non-violent feminist resistance against nuclear weapons, faced a significant setback as women activists were forcibly removed from the site.**

● **Austin Rover reveals its new Montego four-door saloon which replaces the Austin Ambassador and Morris Ital and is derived from the Maestro hatchback.**

Car enthusiasts also eagerly anticipated the launch of its five-door estate version, expected to hit the roads later that year.

Events that took place in the US

● **The 56th Academy Awards, hosted by Johnny Carson, are held at the Dorothy Chandler Pavilion.**

Amidst a sea of talent and artistry, "Terms of Endearment" stood out, winning the coveted Best Picture award.

● **Margaret Heckler of the US General Health Service identifies HTLV-III as the virus that causes AIDS, marking a significant step forward in understanding and eventually combating the devastating disease.**

● An earthquake hits California: The shock had a moment magnitude of 6.2 and a maximum Mercalli intensity of VIII (Severe).

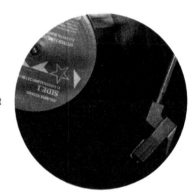

● After 37 weeks Michael Jackson's album Thriller is knocked off the top album spot by Footloose.

More than 70 inches of snow falls on Red Lake Montana - enough to cover a human being!

EVENTS THAT TOOK PLACE IN MAY

Top Songs across the UK and USA charts this month:

United States: Against All Odds - Phil Collins
United Kingdom: The Reflex - Duran Duran

Events that took place in the UK

● **The Liverpool International Garden Festival opens.**

The festival was hugely popular, attracting 3,380,000 visitors.

● **The Thames Barrier, designed to shield the historic city of London from the threat of floods, ensuring the safety and preservation of its iconic landmarks is opened by the Queen.**

● **The Orgreave colliery became a battleground as striking miners and police clashed in a violent confrontation.**

Arthur Scargill, the fiery leader of the miners, is arrested and accused of obstruction.

Everton wins the FA Cup, their first significant trophy for fourteen years with a 2–0 win over Watford in the final at Wembley Stadium.

Liverpool FC secures a third consecutive league title and the fifteenth in the club's history, in spite of being held to a 0–0 draw away at Notts County.

Liverpool wins the European Cup for the fourth time and are the first English club to win three major trophies in the same season.

Events that took place in the US

● 1984 Summer Olympics boycott: the Soviet Union reports that it will boycott the 1984 Summer Olympics in Los Angeles, California.

They gave their reason as concerns over the safety of their athletes in what they called an anti-communist environment.

● Michael Silka murders nine individuals near Manley Hot Springs, Alaska.

29

The 1984 Louisiana World Expo opens in New Orleans, drawing visitors to the vibrant heart of the Crescent City for a unique blend of music, food and global camaraderie.

The Edmonton Oilers rout the New York Islanders to win their first ever Stanley Cup.

Six death row detainees in Virginia escape prison.

Their taste of freedom was short-lived, however, as they were swiftly recaptured.

EVENTS THAT TOOK
PLACE IN JUNE

Top Songs across the UK and USA charts this month:

United States: Let's Hear It For The Boy - Deniece Williams
United Kingdom: Wake Me Up Before You Go-go - Wham

Events that took place in the UK

British unemployment is at a record high of around 3.2 Million. This underscored the pressing need for economic reforms and job creation strategies.

One hundred and twenty individuals are arrested when fighting breaks out outside the Houses of Parliament during a mass lobby by striking miners.

● Austin Rover unveiled its latest automotive marvel, the Rover 200 Series saloon.

In a move set to reshape the British education landscape, the government announced the phasing out of O-level and CSE tests.

In their place, the GCSE was introduced. The first GCSE courses are set to start in September 1986.

The European Parliament Election is held.
The Conservatives lead the way with 45 MEPs, with Labour runner-up with 32. However, the SDP-Liberal Alliance faced a setback, failing to win a single MEP seat.

The debut trip of the first Virgin Atlantic plane takes place, marking the beginning of Richard Branson's ambitious foray into the aviation industry.

Control of London Transport is taken away from the Greater London Council and moved to London Regional Transport (answering to the Secretary of State for Transport) under the terms of the London Regional Transport Act.

Events that took place in the US

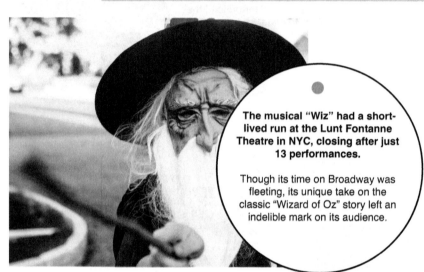

The musical "Wiz" had a short-lived run at the Lunt Fontanne Theatre in NYC, closing after just 13 performances.

Though its time on Broadway was fleeting, its unique take on the classic "Wizard of Oz" story left an indelible mark on its audience.

In a ground-breaking scientific achievement, DNA is effectively cloned from an extinct creature.

NASA faced a significant challenge when a vehicle malfunction occurred during the launch of Intelsat 509.

34

Bruce Springsteen, the iconic rock legend, released his seventh studio album "Born in the USA" which became a defining soundtrack of the 1980s.

The US Supreme Court made a landmark ruling, stating that evidence acquired unlawfully could still be admitted in court if it could be demonstrated that the evidence would have been discovered through legal means.

This sparked debates on the balance between individual rights and the pursuit of justice.

American fighter Thomas Hearns holds the WBC light middleweight title with the second round KO of Roberto Durán of Panama at Caesar's Palace, Las Vegas.

35

EVENTS THAT TOOK PLACE IN JULY

Top Songs across the UK and USA charts this month:

United States: The Reflex - Duran Duran
United Kingdom: Two Tribes - Frankie goes to Hollywood

Events that took place in the UK

In a move reflecting changing societal views on pet ownership, there was a proposal to abolish dog licensing.

The tenth G7 summit is held in London, bringing together leaders from the world's major economies.

These gatherings are pivotal in shaping global economic policies and fostering international cooperation.

Robert Maxwell, a towering figure in the media world, made headlines by acquiring the Daily Mirror for a whopping £113.4 million.

The magazine "Tit-Bits," a staple in British popular culture for over a century, closed its pages after 104 years.

The tranquillity of the Llŷn Peninsula in North Wales was disrupted by a magnitude 5.4 seismic earthquake.

The effects of this quake reverberated across the UK.

● Neil Kinnock's hopes of getting to be Prime Minister are given a lift by the most recent MORI survey which puts Labour three points in front of the Conservatives.

● Great Britain and Northern Ireland win 5 gold, 11 silver and 21 bronze medals at the Los Angeles Olympics.

Events that took place in the US

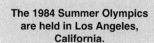

The 1984 Summer Olympics are held in Los Angeles, California.

Vanessa L. Williams becomes the first Miss America to resign when she gives up her crown. Her decision came in the wake of a scandal involving explicit photographs published in Penthouse magazine.

Drama Santa Clause Barbara débuts on NBC TV.

The show revolves around the eventful lives of the wealthy Capwell family of Santa Barbara, California.

The MPAA introduces the PG-13 rating.

This new classification aimed to bridge the gap between PG and R ratings, offering more nuanced guidance to moviegoers.

At the Oak Hill CC, Miller Barber wins the US Senior Open Men's Golf title, edging out the legendary Arnold Palmer by two strokes.

New York Yankees pitcher Phil Niekro strikes out Larry Parish (Texas Rangers) to become the ninth player to achieve the 3,000 MLB strikeout.

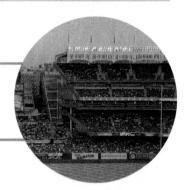

The US passes the National Minimum Drinking Age Act. This legislation mandates a minimum legal drinking age of 21.

EVENTS THAT TOOK PLACE IN AUGUST

Top Songs across the UK and USA charts this month:

United States: When Doves Cry - Prince
United Kingdom: Two Tribes - Frankie goes to Hollywood

Events that took place in the UK

Shoeless South African runner Zola Budd collides with Mary Decker in the 3,000m final at the Olympics.

The incident, which became one of the most talked-about events of the games, unfortunately, meant that neither athlete secured a medal.

A Surrey businessman wins a case in the European Court of Human Rights over illegal phone tapping by the police.

Vauxhall reveals the Mk2 Astra which will go on sale in October.

● **The 1,500m race at the Los Angeles Olympics was a showcase of British athletic prowess.**

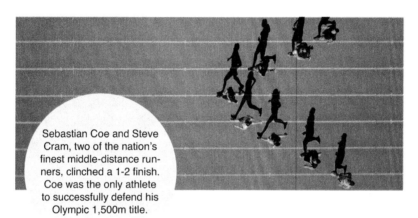

Sebastian Coe and Steve Cram, two of the nation's finest middle-distance runners, clinched a 1-2 finish. Coe was the only athlete to successfully defend his Olympic 1,500m title.

● **Commercial peat-cutters unearthed the preserved body of a man, later dubbed the "Lindow Man," at Lindow Moss in Cheshire. This find provided a rare insight into ancient life and practices in Northwest England.**

● **Star Trek III: The Search For Spock is the leading movie at the Box Office.**

Followed by Indiana Jones and The Temple of Doom.

43

Events that took place in the US

● US President Ronald Reagan, during a voice check for radio broadcast comments, 'My fellow Americans, I'm pleased to tell you today that I've signed legislation that will outlaw Russia forever. We begin bombing in five minutes.' Thankfully, he didn't.

The Space Shuttle Discovery takes off on its first journey, marking a significant milestone in space exploration.

● Amidst global debates on nuclear disarmament and safety, the US conducted nuclear tests in Nevada.

IBM releases PC DOS 3.0. (Personal Computer Disk Operating System) was IBM's version of the MS-DOS operating system.

While many people are familiar with Microsoft's MS-DOS, not everyone realizes that in the early days of personal computing, IBM and Microsoft collaborated.

Jeff Blatnick becomes the first American to win gold in Greco-Roman wrestling at the Los Angeles Olympics.

Having battled and been in remission from Hodgkin's disease, his win was a beacon of hope and resilience.

Prince's "Purple Rain" album not only topped the charts but held its number 1 position for an impressive 24 weeks.

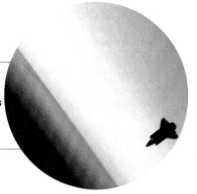

US President Ronald Reagan announced the 'Teacher in Space' initiative, aiming to inspire students by sending educators beyond our planet.

Mary Lou Retton leaped into the history books by becoming the first American female to clinch an Olympic gymnastics medal.

EVENTS THAT TOOK PLACE IN SEPTEMBER

Top Songs across the UK and USA charts this month:

United States: What's Love Got To Do With It - Tina Turner
United Kingdom: Careless Whisper - George Michael

Events that took place in the UK

● **The High Court decides that the miner's strike is unlawful, a setback for all protesters.**

Interesting Fact: An important source of support for the miners came from within their own communities, particularly from the women who set up Women's Action Groups. They organised soup kitchens, distributed food parcels and organised Christmas appeals for miners' families.

● **A MORI survey shows that the Conservatives have a thin lead over Labour for the first time this year.**

Geneticist Alec Jeffreys discovers DNA fingerprinting.

This technique has since been instrumental in solving crimes, reuniting families, and understanding genetic inheritance.

The British monarchy celebrated a joyous occasion as the Princess of Wales gave birth to her second child - Prince Harry.

The United Kingdom and the People's Republic of China consent to return Hong Kong to China in 1997, marking the end of British colonial rule in Hong Kong.

Events that took place in the US

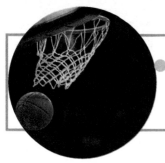

Bruce Sutter of the St Louis Cardinals breaks the record for most saves in a basketball season with his 38th save in a game against the NY Mets.

The "Cosby Show" made its debut on NBC-TV, introducing viewers to the Huxtable family.

The legendary comic Bill Cosby inspired the creation of The Cosby Show with his honest stand-up routines about fatherhood and family in the decades running up to the show's creation.

Elizabeth Taylor, one of the most celebrated actresses of her time, undergoes rehabilitation at the Betty Ford Clinic.

The Space Shuttle Discovery arrives home after embarking on its maiden voyage - a significant step for NASA.

● "Quilters," a musical that weaved together stories of women on the American frontier, opened at the Jack Lawrence Theatre in NYC for 24 performances.

● President Reagan vetoes sanctions against South Africa.

The act banned new U.S. loans and corporate investments in South Africa.

Reagan proposed "constructive engagement" to encourage positive change.

President Ronald Reagan opposed this, believing they would harm the poorest black South Africans and might lead to more civil unrest.

The sanctions impacted South Africa's global relations.

The U.S. decision to impose sanctions was part of a broader global movement against apartheid.

EVENTS THAT TOOK PLACE IN OCTOBER

Top Songs across the UK and USA charts this month:

United States: Let's Go Crazy - Prince & The Revolution
United Kingdom: I Just Called To Say I Love You - Stevie Wonder

Events that took place in the UK

● **David Jenkins, Bishop of Durham voices his concerns over Margaret Thatcher's social policies.**

Factory and mine closures have hit the Durham area since her election as Prime Minister five years ago, damaging the economy.

● Police in Essex make the most significant seizure of cannabis in British criminal history when a multimillion-pound stash of the drug is found on a schooner moored on the River Crouch near North Fambridge village.

Provisional Irish Republican Army targeted the Conservative cabinet with a bombing at a Brighton hotel.

While Prime Minister Margaret Thatcher emerged unscathed, the attack claimed the lives of MP Anthony Berry and four others.

The High Court fines the National Union of Mineworkers £200,000 and Arthur Scargill £1,000 for contempt of court.

Darts player John Lowe achieves the first televised nine-dart finish.

"Thomas the Tank Engine and Friends" makes its debut on ITV.

The television series was based on the beloved children's books by Rev Wilbert Awdry and narrated by Ringo Starr.

The show quickly steamed its way into becoming one of the most cherished children's TV shows ever.

BBC News newsreader Michael Buerk gives TV commentary of the famine in Ethiopia which had already claimed thousands of lives and reportedly had the potential to claim the lives of millions more.

Numerous British charities including Oxfam and Save the Children begin collection work to aid the famine victims.

Events that took place in the US

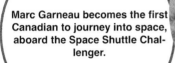

Marc Garneau becomes the first Canadian to journey into space, aboard the Space Shuttle Challenger.

Astronaut Kathryn D. Sullivan becomes the first American female to undertake a spacewalk.

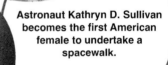

The US government faced an unprecedented shut-down due to disagreements over the passage of bills.

The world of country music came together to honour its best and brightest at the eighteenth Country Music Association Award - Alabama.

NBC unveiled its TV-made movie, "The Burning Bed."

The film, which tackled the harrowing issue of domestic abuse, resonated with audiences and sparked discussions about the societal challenges surrounding the topic.

The Terminator, directed by James Cameron and featuring Arnold Schwarzenegger and Linda Hamilton, is released in the US.

EVENTS THAT TOOK PLACE IN NOVEMBER

Top Songs across the UK and USA charts this month:

United States: Caribbean Queen - Billy Ocean
United Kingdom: Freedom - Wham

Events that took place in the UK

Eight hundred miners end their strike and go back to work after not having enough money to support themselves.

The General Synod of the Church of England supports the appointment of women as deacons, but not as full priests.

British Telecom made financial history with its unprecedented share issue.

As shares went on sale, a staggering two million individuals jumped at the opportunity to buy shares, nearly doubling the number of shareholders in Britain.

British
TELECOM

Thirty-six of Britain and Ireland's top pop stars meet in a Notting Hill studio to form Band Aid and record the song 'Do They Know It's Christmas?' to raise funds to stop starvation in Ethiopia.

The song was written by Bob Geldof and Midge Ure. Upon its release, it became one of the best-selling singles of all time in the UK, and its success led to the creation of the Live Aid concerts the following year, further raising awareness and funds for famine relief in Ethiopia.

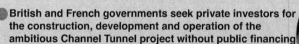

British and French governments seek private investors for the construction, development and operation of the ambitious Channel Tunnel project without public financing

THE EVENTS THAT HAPPENED IN 1984

 Events that took place in the US

The Unemployment Rate takes a positive turn, dropping to 7.2%, a rate similar to the point at which the mid-1980s recession began in June 1981.

The 1984 United States presidential election saw Ronald Reagan secure a decisive victory over Walter F. Mondale, with Reagan garnering 59% of the popular vote.

Cesar Chavez, a stalwart advocate for the rights of farm workers and Hispanics, delivered a poignant speech titled 'What's on the Horizon for Farm Workers and Hispanics?' at the Commonwealth Club in San Francisco.

In Raleigh, North Carolina, convicted murderer Velma Barfield becomes the first woman in the United States to be executed since 1962.

Anna Fisher becomes the first mother to go into orbit when she launches on NASA mission STS-51A.

Horror film A Nightmare on Elm Street is released in the United States.

In a symbolic gesture of recognition and respect, William Penn, the founder of Pennsylvania, was posthumously conferred the title of Honorary Citizen of the United States, over 250 years after his passing.

EVENTS THAT TOOK PLACE IN DECEMBER

Top Songs across the UK and USA charts this month:

United States: Wake Me Up Before You Go-go - Wham
United Kingdom: I Should Have Known Better - Jim Diamond

Events that took place in the UK

● **British Telecom, once a state-owned entity, underwent a significant transformation as it was privatised.**

Post-privatisation, the telecommunications market in the UK was opened up to competition. Before privatisation, BT had a monopoly on telecommunications services. After privatisation, regulatory measures were put in place to ensure fair competition, leading to the emergence of various other providers.

The Band Aid charity single 'Do They Know It's Christmas' is released and goes straight to the top of the UK charts.

● Mikhail Gorbachev's visit to Britain signified strengthening ties and diplomatic dialogues between the UK and the Soviet Union.

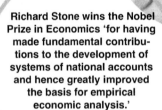

Richard Stone wins the Nobel Prize in Economics 'for having made fundamental contributions to the development of systems of national accounts and hence greatly improved the basis for empirical economic analysis.'

César Milstein, along with Niels Kaj Jerne and Georges J. F. Köhler, was recognized with the Nobel Prize in Physiology or Medicine. Their groundbreaking work on the immune system and the production of monoclonal antibodies revolutionized medical research and treatments.

Rick Allen, the drummer of Def Leppard loses his left arm in a car crash on the A57.

Allen was determined to continue drumming despite his disability. With the support of his band-mates and the help of engineers, a special electronic drum kit was designed that allowed him to use foot pedals to trigger drum sounds that he previously would have played with his left arm.

Events that took place in the US

● NASA intentionally crashes a remote-controlled Boeing 720. This was a calculated move to gather data and insights that could enhance aviation safety and improve aircraft design.

● Beverly Hills Cop, directed by Martin Brest and featuring Eddie Murphy and Judge Reinhold, debuts in Los Angeles.

The film quickly solidified Eddie Murphy's status as a leading man in Hollywood.

American fighter Greg Page knocks out Gerrie Coetzee in the eighth round to win WBA heavyweight title in Sun City, South Africa.

American tennis icon Chris Evert wins her 1,000th career professional match, beating Pascale Paradis of France 6–1, 6–7, 6–2 in round 16 at the Australian Open.

Not only did she secure this landmark victory, but she also went on to clinch the Australian Open title, further cementing her legacy in the sport.

67

THE BEST AND THE WORST
1984 HAD TO OFFER

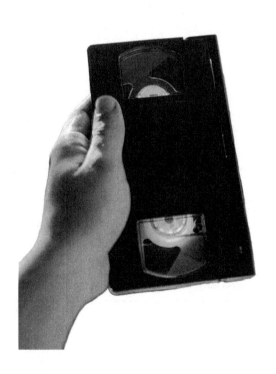

Reagan re-elected in landslide election; Walter Mondale is never heard from again.

The first all rap radio format is introduced at LA's KDAY.

 The Cosby Show premières.

Stonewashed jeans are introduced.

 The first megabit chip is made at Bell Labs.

Summer Olympics in Los Angeles. The Soviets boycott.

 The first infomercials appear on American TV.

The term cyberspace is coined by William Gibson in his novel Neuromancer.

 Vanessa Williams becomes first African American Miss America.

Michael Jackson's hair caught fire during the shooting of a Pepsi commercial.

 Bob Geldof and Band Aid release "Do They Know It's Christmas?".

TOP MUSIC ALBUMS IN THE US

1. Born In The USA by Bruce Springsteen
2. Purple Rain by Prince
3. Like A Virgin by Madonna
4. Legend, The Best Of Bob Marley by Bob Marley
5. Footloose (soundtrack)
6. Private Dancer by Tina Turner
7. The Unforgettable Fire by U2
8. Make It Big by Wham!
9. Diamond Life by Sade
10. Sports by Huey Lewis & The News

TOP MUSIC ALBUMS IN THE UK

1. The Smiths by The Smiths
2. Reckoning by R.E.M.
3. Ocean Rain by Echo and The Bunnymen
4. The Unforgettable Fire by U2
5. Some Great Reward by Depeche Mode
6. The Top by The Cure
7. Let It Be by The Replacements
8. Treasure by Cocteau Twins
9. Zen Arcade by Hüsker Dü
10. Hyaena by Siouxsie and the Banshees

TOP GROSSING MOVIES IN THE US

1. Beverly Hills Cop
2. Ghostbusters
3. Indiana Jones and the Temple of Doom
4. Gremlins
5. The Karate Kid
6. Police Academy
7. Footloose
8. Romancing the Stone
9. Star Trek III: The Search for Spock
10. Splash

TOP GROSSING MOVIES IN THE UK

1. Ghostbusters
2. Indiana Jones and the Temple of Doom
3. Gremlins
4. Police Academy
5. The Karate Kid
6. Romancing the Stone
7. The Killing Fields
8. Sudden Impact
9. Splash
10. Terms of Endearment

SPORTING HIGHLIGHTS

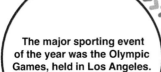

The major sporting event of the year was the Olympic Games, held in Los Angeles.

Winter Olympic Games was held in Sarajevo, Yugoslavia. East Germany finished first on the medals table.

Ivan Lendl won his first grand slam by defeating John McEnroe in French Open.

The Summer Olympics, which was boycotted by the ex-Soviet Union, remains most memorable for the achievements of Carl Lewis who won four gold medals.

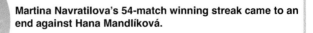

Martina Navratilova's 54-match winning streak came to an end against Hana Mandlíková.

HOW MUCH DID THINGS COST IN 1984?

Yearly inflation rate 4.3%

Yearly inflation rate 5%

A gallon of petrol $1.10

A gallon of petrol £1.83

Average income per year $21,600

Average income per year £10,100

Average cost of new house £37,182

Average cost of new house $86,730

Average monthly rent £230

Average monthly rent $375

RENT

POPULAR NAMES
(IS YOURS HERE?)

Nicole   Jennifer

Sarah

Ashley   Stephanie

Heather

Elizabeth

Melissa   Jessica   Amanda

Christopher   Daniel

James   Matthew   John

Robert

David

Joseph

Joshua   Michael

AND OF COURSE...

YOU!

HAPPY BIRTHDAY!

THANKS FOR MAKING 1984 SO SPECIAL!

THE EVENTS
THAT HAPPENED IN
1984

THE END.

KNOW SOMEONE WHO WOULD LOVE THIS BOOK?

GET THEM A COPY!

Printed in Great Britain
by Amazon

44644525R00046